MORE BAKING
with Schmecks Appeal

EDNA STAEBLER

McGraw-Hill Ryerson
Toronto   Montreal

McClelland & Stewart
Toronto

More Baking with Schmecks Appeal

Copyright © 1991 by Edna Staebler

First published in 1991 by

McGraw-Hill Ryerson Limited
300 Water Street
Whitby, Canada
LlN 9B6

McClelland & Stewart Limited
481 University Avenue
Suite 900
Toronto, Canada
M5G 2E9

1 2 3 4 5 6 7 8 9 10 W 0 9 8 7 6 5 4 3 2 1

Canadian Cataloguing in Publication Data

Staebler, Edna, date.
   More baking with schmecks appeal

(Schmecks appeal cookbook series)
ISBN: 0-7710-8274-6

1. Baking.   2. Bread.   3. Cookery, Mennonite.
4. Cookery — Ontario — Waterloo (Regional municipality).
I. Title.   II. Series: Staebler, Edna, date. The schmecks appeal cookbook series.

TX769.S83   641.8'15   C90-095547-3

This book was manufactured using acid-free paper.

Printed and bound in Canada

CONTENTS

BISCUITS

You won't starve or be at a loss to serve unexpected guests if you have the makings of biscuits in your cupboard; flour, baking powder, shortening, and liquid will make a substitute for bread. You don't need much equipment either: an oven or griddle, a bowl, and a spoon; if you don't have a rolling pin, you can use a wine bottle, flatten the dough with your hands, or drop blobs of it on a cookie sheet.

From the Basic Biscuits recipe (page 3) you can make an infinity of variations. That's when you have fun. You can't fool around much with cake recipes. Cakes must rise and stay risen, so must muffins. But who's to know if biscuits were supposed to be fat or flaky? If you put in good ingredients, they'll taste good.

You can't miss: you can try almost anything and get away with it. The secret is not to apologize if your biscuits aren't fat. Simply serve them, say nothing, and wait cheerfully for a positive reaction from your guests. If you don't get it, if they don't eat voraciously, you might explain that some biscuits are supposed to be thin, solid, or what have you. They really are.

Next time you make biscuits, follow a recipe exactly or venture again and hope for better luck.

I'd like to write in full all the variations I can think of, but if I did I wouldn't have room for all the other recipes in this book, so I must let you experiment by yourself. Every time you get a winner, write it down so you can make it again — and again.

Don't be afraid to experiment. Just remember to be sensible: you have to put certain things in a bowl that together will do what you want them to. You must use flour, a leavening agent, and liquid. Otherwise your guests will require canine teeth to eat the biscuits.

But what's wrong with making dog biscuits? Somebody has to do it. The only excuse you need is a dog.

BISCUIT INFORMATION

In my kitchen I have a deep drawer I frequently refill with 22-pound bags of all-purpose flour. That is the only flour I use in all my recipes unless I specify otherwise.

Roll biscuit dough to ⅛-inch thick and cut with a tuna tin or cookie cutter about 3 inches in diameter. If you want crusty biscuits, roll the dough thinner and cut biscuits smaller; if you want them softer and flaky, roll the dough thicker, cut the biscuits larger and place them close together on a buttered cookie sheet. Or simply drop a large spoonful of dough on a sheet.

Biscuits may seem more bother to make than muffins because the dough is usually rolled out instead of being dropped into muffin cups, but a flat cookie sheet is easier to butter and there is no fear that the biscuits won't come off all in one piece — a slight hazard with muffins, as I have discovered a few times.

Biscuits can be prepared ahead and refrigerated for 48 hours before baking; when baked, they can be frozen and kept for 6 months. But why would you?

To reheat for serving, place the biscuits in a toaster oven, a microwave, or a heavy pot, covered, at low heat on top of the stove. Or put them in a brown paper bag, sprinkled with water and bake in a 350°F oven for about 10 minutes.

Basic Biscuits

Biscuits have a standard formula, but you can enjoy experimenting with all sorts of things.

> **2 cups flour**
> **1 tablespoon baking powder**
> **½ teaspoon salt**
> **¼ cup butter or margarine**
> **⅔ or ¾ cup milk**

Sift the flour, baking powder, and salt. Cut in the butter till the mixture is crumbly. Stir in the milk, using just enough to hold everything together. Drop the dough on a floured board, handling it lightly — or kneading it a few times. Roll it about ½ an inch thick and cut it in 2-inch rounds — or be lazy and simply drop tablespoons of the dough on a greased cookie sheet. Bake in a 450°F oven for 12 minutes.

The flavour of this basic recipe can be greatly improved by replacing some of the milk with cream or various juices; an egg or two will give flavour, colour and delicacy.

If you want a sweet dough, add ¼ to ½ a cup of sugar.

You can use buttermilk or sour milk instead of sweet — substituting ½ teaspoon baking soda for 1 teaspoon of the baking powder.

INSPIRATION

These many suggestions are intended merely to give you inspiration. I won't guarantee that all of them will make you the prize-winning baker of the century. But who cares about that? Most prize-winners just get a blue ribbon they don't know what to do with when they get it home. (Pin it to your kitchen curtain.)

The important thing is that you are creating something that might be wonderful, or might not be wonderful — but, above all, will give you enjoyment.

Memorize the Basic Biscuits recipe and keep it in mind while you add or change it to tickle your fancy, to suit an occasion, or simply to satisfy your creative urge. Who knows — you might be a culinary genius. No one will know till you try.

BUTTERMILK TEA BISCUITS

Tender as the night — of a balmy summer. Can be baked in a toaster oven.

>   1½ cups flour
>   1 teaspoon baking powder
>   ½ teaspoon baking soda
>   ½ teaspoon salt
>   ⅓ cup shortening or chicken fat
>   ½ cup plus 2 tablespoons buttermilk

Sift dry ingredients together then blend in shortening till crumbly. (Chicken fat gives the biscuits a lighter texture and more flavour.) Stir in buttermilk till just blended. Drop batter by spoonfuls onto a greased cookie sheet and bake at 450°F for about 7 or 8 minutes or until brown. These featherlight biscuits can be served hot with maple syrup or jam, or eaten with a salad.

FRUITY TEA BISCUITS

This is a super recipe: tasty and tender. You might think it is too big; cut it in half if you want to, but I'll bet you won't cut it a second time. You can always freeze the biscuits if you can't stop eating them.

>   4 cups flour (part whole wheat, optional)
>   1 cup (or less) sugar
>   1 tablespoon baking powder
>   1 teaspoon salt
>   ½ teaspoon baking soda
>   1 cup shortening
>   1 cup orange or mixed peel, or raisins or currants
>   1½ cups buttermilk, or enough to make a firm dough

Sift the dry ingredients; cut in the shortening till well blended (I let my electric beater or food processor do it). Stir in the peel or raisins by hand. Add the buttermilk and stir just long enough to moisten the flour, adding more milk if necessary. Drop large blobs from a tablespoon on an ungreased cookie sheet and bake in a 450°F oven for about 15 minutes, till slightly golden. Serve with a cup of tea.

AUNT ELLIE'S TEA BISCUITS

Aunt Ellie had white hair, mischievous blue eyes, a budgie bird that sat on her head; and she made the best tea biscuits that anyone ever tasted.

4 cups flour
1 cup sugar
1 tablespoon baking powder
1 teaspoon baking soda
1 teaspoon salt
1 cup currants (optional)
1 cup lard or margarine
2 cups buttermilk
Sugar

Mix the dry ingredients and currants and the lard till the mixture is crumbly. Add the buttermilk and mix with a spoon just enough to make sure everything is connected. Drop spoonfuls of the thick dough on a buttered cookie sheet, sprinkle with a bit of sugar and bake in a 400°F oven for about 15 minutes — keep watching till they are golden brown on the edges. Serve them warm; they're so rich they hardly need butter; with the currants in them they don't need jam either.

STRAWBERRY OR PEACH SHORTCAKE

If you want the best strawberry shortcake you've ever tasted, make the dough for Aunt Ellie's Tea Biscuits (omitting the currants). Pat it into a 9" x 13" cake pan, sprinkle the top with white sugar and bake in a 400°F oven for about 30 minutes. Serve warm, smothered with squashed, sugared berries or sliced peaches. Whipped cream, too, if you're not reducing.

SUDDENLY BISCUITS

While Kath was visiting me from Devon, we suddenly needed some biscuits to go with a salad; she noted the ingredients as I whacked them together. Success!

2 cups all-purpose flour
1 cup whole-wheat flour
1 cup bran
¼ cup sugar
1 tablespoon baking powder
1 teaspoon salt
½ teaspoon baking soda
½ cup oil
1 cup (or more) buttermilk

I blended all the dry ingredients, whipped the oil into the buttermilk with a fork until it was creamy, poured it over the flour mixture and stirred it till all the flour was absorbed — no longer. I dropped tablespoonfuls on an ungreased cookie sheet, baked them in a 400°F oven for about 20 minutes and served them hot with butter melting into them.

MAPLE SUGAR BISCUITS

You can't beat the taste of these; and they're easy and fun to do.

2 cups flour
1 tablespoon baking powder
½ teaspoon salt
⅓ cup shortening
1 cup milk
½ cup finely crushed maple sugar

Sift the dry ingredients together, cut in the shortening, then quickly stir in the milk until the dough forms a ball. Knead lightly on a floured surface, then roll to ½-inch thickness. Sprinkle the dough with maple sugar. Fold over and roll to ¾-inch thickness. Now do the same thing again. Cut with a 2- or 3-inch cutter, place on an ungreased baking sheet and bake at 450°F for 12 to 15 minutes.

LIKE HOT CROSS BUNS

Real Hot Cross Buns are made with yeast, but these are faster, easier to make, and a good substitute. You don't have to wait till near Easter to enjoy them.

 2 cups flour
 2 tablespoons sugar
 1 tablespoon baking powder
 ½ teaspoon salt
 2 teaspoons cinnamon
 ½ teaspoon nutmeg
 ¼ teaspoon cloves
 ½ cup butter or margarine
 1 cup raisins
 ½ cup mixed peel
 1 cup milk

 Glaze:
 ½ cup water
 4 tablespoons icing sugar

Sift the dry ingredients together; cut in the butter, stir in the raisins and peel, then the milk. Turn out on a lightly floured surface, pat to 1-inch thickness and cut with a 3-inch cutter. Press a cross on each bun with the back of a knife. Bake on ungreased baking sheets at 425°F for about 12 minutes. While the buns are baking, bring water and icing sugar to a boil, simmer for a minute or two, and as soon as you take the buns from the oven, brush them with the glaze to give them a shine.

LESS BOTHER: Instead of rolling and cutting the dough, simply drop large gobs of it on a cookie sheet. If it isn't near Easter, forget about the crosses and glaze. The buns will be eaten very quickly without. Serve them warm.

MOTHER'S AFTERNOON TEA CAKES

We got only what was left of these after the company ladies had gone home; never enough!

 1½ **cups flour**
 ½ **cup sugar**
 2 **teaspoons baking powder**
 ½ **teaspoon salt**
 ½ **cup butter**
 ½ **cup raisins or currants**
 2 **tablespoons (or more) milk**
 1 **egg, beaten**
 Sugar

Sift the dry ingredients and work in the butter. Add the raisins or currants. Mix lightly into a dough by adding the milk with the egg. Form into small balls, sprinkle with sugar and bake at 375°F till they are slightly browned.

ELLIE'S BAGEL BISCUITS

These are fun to make and good to eat, too. But not with cream cheese and lox like real bagels.

 2 **cups flour**
 ⅓ **cup sugar**
 1½ **teaspoons baking powder**
 ½ **teaspoon salt**
 ¼ **cup butter**
 1 **egg, beaten**
 ⅔ **cup milk or enough to make a firm dough**

Sift the dry ingredients together, then rub in the butter. Stir the beaten egg into the milk, add to the other mixture and mix into a firm dough you can turn on a floured board. Roll to ½-inch thickness and cut into rounds. Drop the rounds — one at a time — into a saucepan full of rapidly boiling water. In about a minute, the biscuit will pop to the surface; immediately remove it with a strainer, drain, and place it on a well-buttered baking sheet. Repeat with the remaining biscuits. Bake for 20 minutes in a 450°F oven. Serve hot, split in half and well buttered — with jam or marmalade.

BUTTERSCOTCH-NUT BISCUITS

These are yummy; not much bother either.

⅓ cup butter, melted
¾ cup packed brown sugar
2 tablespoons cream
1 cup whole pecans or chopped nuts
2 cups flour
2 tablespoons sugar
1 tablespoon baking powder
¾ teaspoon salt
⅓ cup shortening
¾ cup milk

Blend butter, brown sugar, and cream, then put 2 teaspoons in each of 18 well-buttered and floured muffin cups. Sprinkle nuts over mixture in cups. Sift flour, sugar, baking powder, and salt; cut in the shortening. Stir in the milk. Drop the dough into the muffin cups and bake at 425°F for 15 minutes or until golden. Turn out of pans immediately and patch up with the nuts that stuck to the bottom of the pans. No matter.

FLEXIBILITY

After many years of cooking, I have learned to be flexible: to substitute an ingredient I like for one that I don't, or to use something I have for something I haven't, to be able at the last minute to change my menu because there isn't time to make what I'd planned or because someone was going to be late — or early.

I prefer to spend time with my guests instead of with food in the kitchen. I have long since learned not to try to be perfect. I've served some pretty good meals in my day, but quite often my friends have had to be polite about eating things that did not turn out well at all. So what? They always came back with the hope of better luck next time.

Cheese Biscuits

QUICK, SUPER CHEESY BISCUITS

Whenever I want something special to go with a salad — or just to eat with great enjoyment — I whip up a batch of these.

> 1 cup all-purpose flour
> 1 tablespoon baking powder
> ¾ teaspoon salt
> 1 cup whole-wheat flour
> ¼ cup margarine
> 1 cup coarsely grated Cheddar cheese
> ½ cup currants or raisins (optional)
> 1 cup milk

Sift the all-purpose flour, baking powder, and salt, stir in the whole wheat. Cut in the margarine till it disappears. Stir in the cheese and currants. Add the milk, using just enough to hold everything together. Don't handle the dough any more than you need to. Drop gobs of it on an ungreased baking sheet and pop it in a 450°F oven for about 12 minutes. The edges will be golden and you will be unable to resist a quick taste. Don't burn your tongue.

LORNA'S CHEESE DROP BISCUITS

These must be eaten very hot.

> 1 cup flour
> ¼ cup butter
> 2 teaspoons baking powder
> 1 cup grated sharp Cheddar cheese
> ½ cup ice-cold water

Mix the flour, butter, and baking powder like pastry. Add the cheese, then the ice water. Grease a cookie sheet and drop the biscuits from a spoon, about 12. Put a dab of butter on top of each biscuit before baking, at 400°F for 10 to 15 minutes.

PIMENTO CHEESE BISCUITS

These taste as good as they look; try them for company.

2 cups flour
1 tablespoon baking powder
1 teaspoon baking soda
½ teaspoon salt
1 cup shredded sharp Cheddar cheese
2 tablespoons chopped pimento
¼ teaspoon crushed oregano leaves (optional)
1 cup buttermilk

Sift the flour, baking powder, baking soda, and salt together. Stir in the cheese, pimento, and oregano before adding the buttermilk. Turn out onto a floured surface, roll out about ½-inch thick; cut with a floured cutter and place on a greased baking sheet. Bake in a 425°F oven for 15 to 20 minutes. Serve hot.

CHEESE SANDWICH BISCUITS

You'll be tempted to eat several of these at a sitting.

2 cups flour
1 tablespoon baking powder, slightly rounded
½ teaspoon salt
¼ cup shortening
⅔ cup milk, V-8, or tomato juice
Cheese slices
Bacon slices

Sift the dry ingredients together, cut in the shortening until fine, then stir in the milk or juice. Turn dough on a floured board, knead a few times then roll out to about ½-inch thick. Cut into rounds and place thin slices of cheese on half the rounds, covering with the other half. Place on a greased baking sheet, put a small piece of bacon on each biscuit and bake at 450°F until the bacon is crisp and biscuits lightly golden. Serve hot.

CHEESE ROLLS

You don't have to get up early to make these on a Sunday morning; they'll bake while you're cooking the sausages and scrambled eggs.

2 cups flour
1 tablespoon baking powder
1 teaspoon salt
2 tablespoons shortening
¾ cup milk
1 cup grated cheese

Mix and sift the dry ingredients, cut in the shortening and add liquid gradually, mixing to a soft dough. Roll thin on floured board and sprinkle with the cheese. Roll up like a jelly roll, cut in 1-inch pieces and bake on a greased cookie sheet in a 450°F oven for about 12 minutes. These are great, with a luncheon salad — or a cup of afternoon tea.

TO DOUBLE OR HALVE A RECIPE

If you double or halve a recipe, always write the halved or doubled amounts beside the printed figures in the book and be sure to stick to the right column. I've ruined so many things by putting in a full amount of something when all the rest was halved.

Biscuit Rolls

Instead of making plain biscuits, you might want to be a bit fancy. It doesn't take much longer and the taste is well worth the bother. Besides you don't need to serve them with butter and jam.

2 cups flour
1 tablespoon baking powder
½ teaspoon salt
¼ cup butter or margarine
¾ cup milk

Sift the dry ingredients together, cut in the butter, add the milk, and mix until the dough is soft and can be scooped onto a floured surface. Roll out to ⅜-inch thickness. Spread with some soft butter and sprinkle with **½ cup brown sugar**, **cinnamon**, and **raisins**; try **chopped nuts**, **marmalade**, **apple butter**, or **jam** for variety. Roll up like a jelly roll and cut into ½-inch slices; place slices on a well-buttered baking pan and bake at 400°F for about 15 minutes.

CHELSEA ROLLS

Proceed as for Biscuit Rolls, spreading the rolled dough with **soft butter**, **brown sugar**, **raisins**, and **cinnamon**. Melt **¼ cup butter** in a cake pan and sprinkle it with **½ cup brown sugar**. Place biscuit slices in the pan touching each other. Bake at 350°F for about 20 minutes. Carefully invert on a rack. Serve warm.

HONEY OR SYRUP ROLLS

Proceed as for Biscuit Rolls, spreading the rolled dough with **soft butter** and a thin layer of **honey** or **syrup**. Melt and spread **¼ cup butter** in a square cake pan, pour in a thin or thick layer of **honey**, **maple syrup**, or **corn syrup**. Place the biscuit slices close together in the pan and bake at 350°F for about 20 minutes. Invert on a rack over waxed paper and serve warm.

FRUIT ROLLS

Bevvy says these are popular at a barn-raising.

2 cups flour
1 tablespoon baking powder
1½ teaspoons salt
2 tablespoons sugar
2 tablespoons lard
⅔ cup milk or water

Mix in the order given and roll ¼-inch thick. Combine:

2 tablespoons soft butter
½ teaspoon cinnamon
⅓ cup brown sugar
⅓ cup currants

Spread the mixture on the dough, roll like a jelly roll and cut in
¾-inch slices. Place in greased pans and bake in 350°F oven for
15 minutes.

Savoury Biscuits

PIN-WHEEL BISCUITS WITH HERBS

You'll be proud to serve these to your friends with a salad lunch.

½ cup butter, softened
2 tablespoons chopped parsley
Pepper
¼ teaspoon oregano
¼ teaspoon tarragon or your preference
¼ teaspoon thyme
2 cups sifted flour
1 tablespoon baking powder
¾ teaspoon salt
⅓ cup vegetable shortening or oil
¾ cup milk

Whip the butter with the parsley, pepper, and herbs; let stand for an hour or so to blend the flavours. Into a large bowl, sift the flour, baking powder, and salt. Cut in the shortening until the mixture looks like coarse meal. (Easy in a food processor.) Stir in the milk, then turn batter on a floured board and knead about 10 times. Roll out the dough into a rectangle about 10 by 12 inches. Spread with the herb butter and, starting with the 12-inch side, roll up like a jelly roll. Seal the edge. Cut the roll into 24 pinwheels and place them in ungreased muffin pans. Bake at 425°F for 10 to 15 minutes, or until golden. Beautiful and savoury .

SAUSAGE BISCUITS

These are special; read the recipe and see if you don't want to try them as hot hors d'oeuvres or a snack.

> **1 pound sausage meat**
> **2 cups flour**
> **1 tablespoon baking powder**
> **1 teaspoon salt**
> **¼ cup shortening**
> **⅔ cup milk**

Shape all the sausage meat into balls, using a level tablespoon as a measure. Sift the dry ingredients together then cut in the shortening; add the milk and stir to a soft dough. Turn out on a lightly floured surface; knead a few times. Roll dough ¼-inch thick and cut in rounds 3 to 4 inches across. Wrap the rounds around the sausage balls and seal. Place on a greased baking sheet and bake in 375°F oven for about 30 minutes until brown. They can also be served with a sauce or chutney.

KATIE'S SWEET POTATO BISCUITS

Try these some day when you have leftover potatoes.

> **1¼ cups flour**
> **1 tablespoon baking powder, slightly rounded**
> **1 tablespoon sugar**
> **⅓ teaspoon salt**
> **⅔ cup mashed sweet potatoes (or regular potatoes)**
> **⅔ cup milk**
> **3 or 4 tablespoons butter or margarine**

Sift the dry ingredients together. Blend the sweet potatoes, milk, and butter, then stir into the flour mixture to make a soft dough. Turn onto a floured surface and roll to ½-inch thickness; cut with a floured cutter. Place on greased baking sheet and bake in a 450°F oven for about 15 minutes. Serve hot.

ONION SQUARES

A flavoursome treat to be eaten with a salad, soup, or as a snack.

2 cups sliced onions
3 tablespoons butter

Sauté the onions in the butter until they are tender but not brown. Let cool.

2 cups sifted flour
2 teaspoons baking powder
1 teaspoon salt
¼ cup shortening
Sprinkling of your favourite herbs or
    chopped parsley
1 cup milk

Topping:
½ cup grated cheese or ⅓ cup sour cream

Sift the flour, baking powder, and salt together, cut in the shortening until the mixture is fine. Add the herbs or parsley, and milk and stir only until the flour is moistened. Spoon into a well-buttered 8-inch-square pan, spread the sautéed onions over the top and sprinkle with the cheese or slather with sour cream. Bake about 20 minutes in a 425°F oven. Cut in squares and serve hot.

CLARA MAY'S PORK BUNS

In Neil's Harbour I loved to sit on the old rocker beside the big black woodstove and watch Clara May do her baking. So did her grandchildren. She didn't follow a recipe; she couldn't read; nor did she measure anything exactly; she knew by the feel. These are the amounts she told me:

> ¼ **cup salt pork**
> **About 3½ cups flour**
> **2 rounded teaspoons baking powder**
> ½ **teaspoon salt**
> ¼ **cup shortening**
> **1 cup big sticky raisins**
> **1½ cups cold water**

Clara May cut the salt pork into little chunks the size of small peas; she poured boiling water over them and then let them drain while she sifted the flour, baking powder, and salt into a bowl. She cut in the shortening. "You got to work it in with your hands till it feels roight good," she told us. With a fork she stirred in the big sticky raisins and the well-drained pork chunks then poured in about a cupful of cold water. "Stir it till the dough follows the fork around the bowl," she showed us. "Sometimes it needs more water." She gradually added at least another ½ cupful. "Ye want a soft dough but it must hold its shape." She broke off pieces of dough, rolled them around in her hand to a ball and put them on ungreased cookie pans about 1½ inches apart.

Clara May opened the oven door, stuck in her hand to feel. "Henry, the fire needs more wood." She looked round the kitchen. "Where is that man? Lil, go get your father. You want a hot oven for pork buns to get noice and fat and a little bit brown." She answered my question, "How long?" "I don't know, I just look after I wash up the dishes and clean off the table, maybe 10 or 15 minutes."

When the biscuits were baked and cooling on the table, a grandchild reached to take one. "Now you git," Clara May screamed. "I wants them for supper." She put them in tins, then in the cupboard behind the stairs. "If I don't hide 'em," she said, "them grandchildren would have 'em et faster 'n you could skin a codfish."

Biscuits With Toppings

Mix Basic Biscuits dough — which I hope you have memorized (if not, see page 3) — roll the dough ½-inch thick and cut into squares. Place squares, touching each other, on a buttered sheet with sides or a large cake pan. Sprinkle over them a mixture of **½ teaspoon cinnamon** mixed with **½ cup white or brown sugar, chopped nuts and⁄or raisins**; drizzle with **¼ cup melted butter.** You could vary the topping by using coffee cake toppings (pages 52-53), jam or cherries, or whatever you think would be pleasant. Bake at 400°F for about 15 minutes.

Coated Biscuits

These are fun to make and present many possibilities.

Make the Basic Biscuits dough (page 3), pat a tablespoon or so of dough into a ball, flatten it a little, then roll it in **melted butter** then in **breadcrumbs** blended with **grated cheese.** Bake in a 350°F oven for about 20 minutes — but watch it. Cool on a rack and eat warm.
Or sprinkle the butter-coated biscuits with finely cut herbs.
Or chopped sauteed onions.
Or sprinkle the butter coated biscuits with sesame or poppy seeds.
Or finely chopped nuts.

Now you see what I mean about creating biscuits with variations. From now on you are on your own — with no limitations.

FLAVOURED BUTTERS

Instead of serving hot biscuits with butter and jam, you could simply prepare the following butters to spread on the biscuits when you serve them. The butters can be stored in covered jars in your fridge or freezer but should be softened before you use them.

MAPLE BUTTER

Every spring when the sap is running Hannah, Eva, and Almeda make maple butter of pure maple syrup very carefully kept at a certain temperature and beaten an exact length of time in an electric mixer. They pour it into containers which they keep or sell at the markets. It is a wonderful treat to eat spread on biscuits, muffins, or toast. Unless you have know-how, the equipment and the syrup, I'd advise you to try something easier — though it won't be nearly as pure and good. Try this:

Cream **½ cup butter or margarine** until soft then slowly beat in **2 tablespoons or more maple syrup** until the mixture is light and fluffy. You can see why it wouldn't be as wonderful as Eva and Hannah's.

HONEY BUTTER

Add **¼ cup liquid honey** to **½ cup butter or margarine** and beat until light.

JAM BUTTER

Cream until soft **½ cup butter or margarine**, add **¼ cup jam or marmalade** and beat until light.

ORANGE OR LEMON BUTTER

Add **2 tablespoons orange or lemon juice** and **1 tablespoon finely grated rind** to **½ cup creamed butter or margarine** and beat until light.

EVER-READY PEEL — ORANGE, LEMON, OR GRAPEFRUIT

How often do you come across a recipe that requires a tablespoon or so of grated peel? Do you always have it? I do. Whenever I buy oranges with thin soft peel — navel, temple, or tangerines — I peel them, put the peel in a plastic bag in the freezer of my kitchen fridge and I always have orange peel whenever I need it.

When a recipe calls for a bit of orange rind — or a lot of it — I take what I want out of the bag, pop some into my blender, give it a whirl till the peel is finely chopped; sometimes I add the liquid that is part of the recipe to get better results. It's all so easy, the orange tastes fresh and is always available when oranges aren't.

STRAWBERRY BUTTER

This is a very special treat you can make during the strawberry season to spread on hot biscuits, scones, hot cakes, or toast.

**2 or 3 ripe strawberries (the number depends
  on the ripeness and size)
½ cup softened butter
1 teaspoon lemon juice**

Crush the berries and beat them into the softened butter with the lemon juice until smooth. That's it! Store it in a pretty little pottery jar with a lid in your fridge, or spread it on wax paper and shape it into a roll 1½ inches in diameter. If the mixture is too soft, chill it before shaping. Store the roll in the fridge and cut in slices to spread.

MOCK HONEY

This recipe came from Melvin Baumann's grandmother. Eva says she's never tried it because she's always had plenty of honey, but if you have a lawnful of clover and a couple of roses it might be fun to experiment. I guarantee nothing.

**5 pints sugar
½ teaspoon ground alum
3 cups hot water
Petals of 2 roses
18 red clover flowers
30 white clover flowers**

Put sugar, alum, and water in a saucepan on the stove and boil 4 minutes — no longer or it will get too thick. Pour this over the separated petals and flowers. Let stand 15 minutes then strain and put in sterilized jars. That's beating the bees.

Savoury Butters

To give added flavour and zest, you can spread the following easily made butters over unsweet biscuits, bread, toast, English muffins, sandwiches, crackers, hot dog or hamburger buns, or serve on fish, pork or lamb chops, beef steaks, meat patties, baked potatoes, tomatoes, broccoli, cauliflower, carrots, peas, onions. Be courageous: experiment.

Simply blend thoroughly whatever flavour or combination of flavours you like with **½ cup soft butter or margarine**. A teaspoon of lemon juice, sherry, or mustard might make some taste even better. The choice is yours.

GARLIC BUTTER

The favourite — **1 to 3 cloves garlic, finely minced, or 1 teaspoon garlic salt**.

ONION BUTTER

Two tablespoons finely minced onion or **onion soup mix**, or **1 teaspoon onion salt** — but watch it because it might be too salty.

CURRY BUTTER

One-half **teaspoon curry powder** and a **dash of pepper**.

HERB BUTTER

One teaspoon dry herbs or **2 tablespoons finely chopped fresh herbs**. You might try parsley, chives, tarragon, thyme, basil, or anything you like.

CELERY BUTTER

One teaspoon celery seeds, ¼ teaspoon pepper and **paprika**.

SAVOURY BUTTER

Try adding **Worcestershire sauce, or chili sauce, chutney, Marmite**, beef bouillon extract, **or tomato paste**. How much you add to the butter is up to you — but don't overdo it.

SCONES, BANNOCKS, HOT CAKES, AND POPOVERS

Scones and bannocks are pioneer cousins to a biscuit. A bannock is baked whole in a large round or oval; a scone is rolled out round and cut like a pie into triangles that are baked separately. In Scotland, both are baked on a "girdle," or griddle, or in a hot, heavy frying pan, over slow heat until the bottom is browned. They are then turned over and browned on the other side. The same baking is done with hot cakes.

Of course, the safest way is to be conventional and bake scones, bannocks, and hot cakes in a proper hot oven until browned.

About popovers I'll tell you later.

Scones

CAPE BRETON SCONES

"And these are some good," anyone in Neil's Harbour will tell you.

2 cups flour
2 tablespoons sugar
1 tablespoon baking powder
1 teaspoon salt
¼ teaspoon baking soda
1 cup raisins or currants
½ cup sour cream
¼ cup oil
1 egg, slightly beaten
3 tablespoons milk

Sift together the dry ingredients and stir in the raisins. Blend the remaining ingredients and stir into the flour mixture until the dough is all together. Toss on a lightly floured surface until no longer sticky. Knead a few times. Divide the dough in half, then pat each ball of dough to a 6-inch circle with the top slightly rounded. Brush the tops with milk, and sprinkle with sugar. Cut each circle into 6 wedges. Place 2 inches apart on a cookie sheet. Bake at 425°F for 10 to 12 minutes or until golden. Serve hot with butter and jam or flavoured butter or honey .

BEING PREPARED

For people who drop in without any notice I always have cookies in my cookie jar and a few frozen muffins or biscuits that I can put into my toaster oven to serve with a potful of tea. If people call me from town and say they'll be out right away, I know it will be half an hour and I'll have time to stir up some muffins, a coffee cake, or a quick bread. When they arrive, they say, "My it smells good in here." And I welcome them.

SCOTTISH SCONES

Quick and easy to make — and to eat.

>2 cups flour
>½ cup sugar
>1 tablespoon baking powder, slightly rounded
>1 teaspoon salt
>5 tablespoons shortening
>½ cup currants
>⅔ cup milk

Sift the dry ingredients together, then cut in the shortening thoroughly. Add the currants and stir in the milk. Turn out on a floured board and knead a bit. Pat out to ¾-inch thickness and cut into 4-inch rounds. Place on a buttered baking sheet and bake at 450°F until golden. Split and butter while hot.

MARTINA SCHNEIKER'S SCONES

Martina says she can never make enough of these.

>3 cups sifted flour
>1 cup sugar
>2 teaspoons baking powder
>1 teaspoon salt
>¾ cup butter or margarine
>1 cup raisins
>1 egg, well beaten
>Milk, almost a cupful

>*Topping:*
>1 egg yolk, beaten
>2 tablespoons milk

Sift the dry ingredients into a bowl. Cut the butter into the mixture until it is fine, add the raisins and mix well. Beat an egg in a measuring cup, add enough milk to fill the cup, stir into the flour mixture. Knead lightly, roll out to a dinner-plate-size round. Cut into triangles. Brush tops with a beaten egg yolk blended with 2 tablespoons of milk. Bake at 450°F for 10 to 12 minutes. Eat warm.

WHOLE WHEAT SCONES

This recipe was given to me by a Schmecks fan who lives in British Columbia. There are some good cooks out there in the west.

3⅓ cups whole-wheat flour
½ teaspoon baking soda
¼ cup butter
2 eggs
1½ tablespoons honey — or more
½ cup raisins — or more
1 cup milk
1 tablespoon lemon juice

Sift the flour and soda together and cut in the butter. Beat the eggs, add the honey, raisins, milk, and lemon juice, then mix well with the flour. Add more milk if the dough is too dry to roll to a ¾-inch thickness. Cut into triangles and place on lightly greased baking sheet. Bake in a 425°F oven for about 20 minutes. Serve hot.

HOT GINGER SCONES

Easy to make and very good with applesauce.

2 cups flour
1 tablespoon baking powder
2 teaspoons ground ginger
⅛ teaspoon salt
2 tablespoons shortening
¾ cup milk
2 tablespoons corn syrup

Sift together the dry ingredients; cut in the shortening, then stir in lightly the milk which has been blended with the corn syrup. Drop tablespoons of the batter on a greased cookie sheet and bake at 425°F for about 15 minutes.

Hot Cakes

SINGIN' HINNIES

These are a Cape Breton treat. You'll feel like singin' too when you try them.

> **4 cups flour**
> **2 teaspoons sugar**
> **1 teaspoon baking soda**
> **2 teaspoons cream of tartar**
> **Pinch of salt**
> **¼ cup lard**
> **¼ cup margarine**
> **1¼ cup currants, or currants and sultanas mixed**
> **2 tablespoons milk — or enough to make a fairly stiff dough**

Mix flour, sugar, baking soda, cream of tartar, and salt, then rub in the lard and margarine. Add currants and milk to make a dough just stiff enough to roll ¾-inch thick. Cut into thick rounds and bake on a greased griddle or lightly greased electric frying pan set low, until brown. Turn and cook on other side. Split and spread with butter and jam. Then sing a Scottish song.

PHILIP'S WELSH CAKES

Every year on Saint David's Day, Philip's mother made Welsh Cakes. Stored in a covered container they kept well for a long time — unless Philip found where they were hidden.

3 cups flour
⅔ cup sugar
1½ teaspoons baking powder
1 teaspoon salt
½ teaspoon baking soda
½ teaspoon nutmeg
¼ teaspoon mace
1 cup butter, margarine, or lard
½ cup finely chopped mixed peel
¾ cup currants
2 eggs, beaten
⅓ cup milk, more or less

Sift the dry ingredients together and cut in the butter. Add the fruit, then the eggs mixed with milk to make a stiff dough. On a floured surface roll out half the dough to ¼-inch thickness; cut into rounds with a 2- or 3-inch cookie cutter. Do the same with the other half of the dough. Bake on a heated griddle at low heat, or an electric frying pan set at 250°F for 8 to 10 minutes. When puffy and golden on one side, turn and bake second side until golden. Serve hot or cold with butter.

QUICK HOT CAKES

Make these for breakfast on Sunday morning and you will be blest.

> **2½ cups flour**
> **1 tablespoon baking powder — slightly rounded**
> **½ teaspoon salt**
> **¼ cup shortening**
> **1 cup milk or water**
> **Additional flour**

Sift the dry ingredients together, cut in the shortening then stir in the milk. Place the dough on a floured board; knead a bit. Roll out ¼-inch thick and cut with a round cutter. Sprinkle about 1 tablespoon additional flour on griddle over low heat. When the flour is lightly browned, place the cakes on the griddle, with space between each. Cook until brown on both sides. Repeat with remaining cakes. Serve hot with bacon and eggs, butter and jam, or flavoured butter.

ANYONE'S SOUR CREAM HOTCAKES

I don't remember who gave me this recipe, I only know it's a good one.

> **2 tablespoons flour**
> **2 tablespoons sugar**
> **¼ teaspoon baking soda**
> **Pinch of salt**
> **2 eggs, beaten**
> **1 cup sour cream**

Sift the dry ingredients together; add the eggs blended with the cream and mix well. Spoon onto a hot griddle and turn once to brown on both sides. Serve with syrup, jam, or sauce.

Bannocks

CAPE BRETON BANNOCK (with my options)

In their home on the edge of the sea at Neil's Harbour, Archie and Irene Walker had lots of visitors; Irene said this bannock was her standby. No wonder they had lots of visitors. Combine the following:

> **1½ cups bran**
> **1½ cups flour (1 whole wheat, ½ white)**
> **1½ teaspoons salt**
> **½ cup wheat germ (optional)**
> **1 teaspoon baking soda**
> **1 teaspoon baking powder**
> **2 tablespoons brown sugar**
> **2 handfuls coconut**

Cut in with a knife:

> **¼ cup oil (or more)**

Add my options if you like:

> **1 cup sunflower seeds, or**
> **1 cup raisins or currants**

Stir in:

> **1½ cups buttermilk, or more**
> **to make a firm dough**

Gently form dough into a large ball and place it on a buttered pan; press it out to an oval 1- or 1½-inches thick. Cut a cross on top for good luck, and bake at 400°F until it is toasty brown — Irene said 45 minutes but mine was done in 20. Cut it in squares or simply break off pieces.

JEAN SALTER'S OATMEAL BANNOCKS

Crisp and toasty to eat with cheese or fruit; very popular.

> **3½ cups quick oats**
> **1 teaspoon salt**
> **2 tablespoons flour**
> **½ cup shortening**
> **About ½ cup water**

Combine the oats, salt, and flour. Cut in the shortening and add enough water to dampen and form a ball. (A food processor does this in a jiffy.) Leave to swell for 10 minutes. Divide the dough in two and roll each part to ⅛-inch thickness; slide onto an ungreased cookie sheet, indent into squares with a pastry wheel or knife. Bake in a 350°F oven for about ½ an hour, but watch that they don't turn brown.

SWEET OATMEAL COOKIES

Jean says just add **1 cup sugar** to the bannock recipe.

Popovers

When I was married — two-thirds of my life ago — I had to teach myself how to cook. One of the first things I tackled successfully was popovers. They were so easy and they never failed to rise miraculously and stay risen. I proudly served them with butter and homemade chokecherry jelly or strawberry jam to whatever couple we'd invited to our house on a Friday evening to play bridge with us. It may have seemed a rather odd choice of refreshment, but at that time in my life I had never baked a cake or even a muffin and wasn't sure that I could.

I used the cold-oven method of making popovers because I could mix the batter before my guests came, half-fill greased custard cups — or muffin tins — and put them into the cold oven. Before we played our last rubber of bridge I turned the oven to 425°F, and in 45 to 50 minutes, without my looking, the popovers had popped, hollow and high.

    1 cup flour
    1 cup milk
    2 large eggs
    1 tablespoon melted butter or oil
    ½ teaspoon salt

Measure all the ingredients into a bowl and beat and beat until the mixture is smooth, smooth as thick cream. Pour into greased muffin pans — not more than half full — or into custard cups. Bake as I've told you above or preheat the oven to 375°F and bake the popovers for 50 minutes or bake them at 400°F for 35 to 40 minutes. But don't peek. The secret is in leaving them alone. Serve them hot and immediately.

POPOVER VARIATIONS

After you've made a few hundred popovers and served them with butter and jam, you might like to try them, instead of patty shells, as containers for almost anything creamed: chicken, shellfish, tuna or salmon. They make a great lunch with a salad.

For breakfast you could fill popover shells with scrambled eggs.

For dessert you could try adding a teaspoon of sugar or honey to the batter and then fill the baked popovers with sugared fresh fruit — strawberries and peaches are really special — topped with whipped cream.

COFFEE CAKES

Want to try baking something that is easy, delicious, and almost foolproof? Make a coffee cake. Except for muffins, a coffee cake is probably the best thing you can whip up in a hurry — and it's much less bother than a cake. A coffee cake takes only a few minutes to mix, 30 minutes to bake; with a baked-on topping it is ready to be eaten as soon as it comes from the oven — hot with morning coffee, brunch, lunch, or afternoon tea, served as a dessert with supper or as a bedtime snack. It can be enjoyed hot or cold, today or tomorrow, frozen and reheated whenever you need it.

Do you have sour cream in your fridge that is just past its prime, or buttermilk, sour milk, or milk powder? Coffee cakes are versatile. You can vary the toppings till you've hit the combination you like best, then bask in the praise that will come your way. You can't fail; the only disaster that might befall a coffee cake is that the topping might sink into the batter. And what if it does? The flavour will still be there, perhaps enhanced, and if you don't mention it, who's to know that it wasn't intended? Some coffee cakes are supposed to be made that way.

Good luck, have fun, and if you try these recipes I know you'll have good eating I tried more than forty coffee cakes during the past year and I think these are the best.

BUTTERMILK COFFEE CAKE

Easy to make, tender — and everyone wants the recipe, Bevvy tells me.

> **2¼ cups flour**
> **1 teaspoon salt**
> **1½ teaspoons cinnamon**
> **1 cup brown sugar, firmly packed**
> **¾ cup granulated sugar**
> **¾ cup lard**
> **½ cup walnuts, coarsely chopped**
> **1 teaspoon baking soda**
> **1 teaspoon baking powder**
> **1 egg, slightly beaten**
> **1 cup buttermilk or sour cream**

Sift flour with salt and ½ teaspoon of cinnamon into a large bowl. Add sugars and lard and mix until all is well blended and feathery (use your electric mixer). Take out ¾ cup of this mixture for topping and to it add the nuts and the remaining 1 teaspoon of cinnamon; mix and set aside. To the remaining mixture, add baking soda, baking powder, egg, and buttermilk; mix until smooth. Spoon mixture into a greased 9" x 9" pan, sprinkle the reserved topping over it and press it down lightly. Bake in a 350°F oven for about 30 minutes — or until it tests done. Cut into squares and serve warm or cold. It is moist and tender and wonderful (even if it drops in the middle as mine did the first time I tried it).

NO PROBLEM

My Mother was a wonderful cook; everything she made had a wonderful flavour. She used lots of butter, sugar or whatever she thought was needed to make a recipe better. No one taught Mother how to cook or to bake; she always maintained that you needed only to be able to read a recipe to be able to make it.

Can you read? Then you'll have no problem. You simply do what a recipe tells you to do. That's a good way to start till you develop an instinct that tells you what changes you can make and still have good results.

ORANGE STREUSEL COFFEE CAKE

This really is one of the best. It should serve twelve but three of us ate almost all of it with our tea one afternoon.

2 cups flour
½ cup sugar
2½ teaspoons baking powder
½ teaspoon salt
Grated rind of 1 orange, or more
1 egg, slightly beaten
½ cup milk
½ cup orange juice
⅓ cup oil

Streusel:
¼ cup flour
¼ cup sugar
2 tablespoons grated orange rind, or more
2 tablespoons butter or margarine

Sift flour, sugar, baking powder, and salt; stir in orange rind. Make a well in the centre and pour in egg, milk, orange juice, and oil. Mix just enough to moisten the flour — the batter should be lumpy. Pour into a 9" x 9" pan. Sprinkle the blended streusel ingredients on top of batter, and bake at 350°F for about 30 minutes, or until slightly brown. If you want to be fancy put a few orange segments on top as decoration.

EGGLESS BUTTERMILK COFFEE CAKE

This is a dandy and you can make it as quick as a flash.

> **2 cups brown sugar**
> **2 cups flour**
> **½ cup butter or margarine**
> **1 teaspoon baking soda**
> **½ teaspoon salt**
> **1 cup buttermilk**
> **½ cup nuts (optional — but nice)**

Mix the sugar, flour, and butter until it has the consistency of fine crumbs. Remove and reserve ½ cup of the mixture for topping. To the remaining flour mixture, add baking soda, salt, and buttermilk; blend well. Spread in a 9" x 9" pan. Sprinkle the reserved crumbs over top (with nuts). Bake at 375°F for 30 minutes, or until a toothpick inserted in the centre comes out clean. (Chopped nuts may be added to the batter as well, if you like.) This freezes well and may be rejuvenated by reheating.

FLORENCE HONDERICH'S SOUR CREAM COFFEE CAKE

Served warm, this is a treat for breakfast — or any time.

> **½ cup butter or margarine**
> **1 cup white sugar**
> **2 eggs, beaten**
> **1 teaspoon vanilla**
> **1 cup sour cream**
> **1 teaspoon baking soda**
> **1 ¾ cups sifted cake flour**
> **2 teaspoons baking powder**
>
> *Topping:*
> **½ cup brown sugar**
> **1 tablespoon cinnamon**
> **½ cup finely chopped nuts**

Blend butter and white sugar, add eggs and vanilla; beat well. Combine sour cream and baking soda (the cream should double in volume but probably won't), add alternately with sifted flour and baking powder to creamed mixture. Spread half the batter in a greased cake pan 9" x 9". Sprinkle with half the topping mixture. Cover with remaining batter and sprinkle the rest of the topping on top. Bake at 350°F for 45 minutes. If there's any left after you serve it, it can be wrapped in foil and reheated.

COFFEE CAKE WITH ROLLED OATS

I made this tempting creation for a visiting male; he preferred three drinks of rye and ginger. I didn't invite him again. The topping with coconut flakes was irresistible. I ate three pieces.

1 cup flour
1 cup brown sugar
½ cup rolled oats
½ cup margarine or butter
½ cup buttermilk
2 eggs
1 teaspoon baking powder
½ teaspoon cinnamon
½ teaspoon salt
¼ teaspoon baking soda
¼ teaspoon nutmeg

Topping:
1 cup chopped nuts
½ cup flaked coconut

Combine flour, sugar, oats, and margarine until crumbly. Reserve ½ cup of crumb mixture for topping. To remaining crumb mix, add remaining ingredients except nuts and coconut. Blend well. Pour batter into greased 8-inch-square or 9-inch-round pan. Sprinkle top with reserved crumbs, nuts and coconut. Bake at 350°F for 25 minutes, or until a toothpick inserted in centre comes out clean. Serve warm or cool with a cup of tea or coffee — never rye and ginger.

RAISIN COFFEE CAKE

Along the edge of this recipe I've noted, "Super flavour, one of the best." But how do I know? I love them all.

2 cups flour
⅔ cup sugar
¾ teaspoon baking powder
¾ teaspoon baking soda
½ teaspoon salt
½ teaspoon nutmeg
1 teaspoon cinnamon
½ cup vegetable oil
1 egg, beaten
½ cup buttermilk or yogourt
⅓ cup corn syrup
½ cup raisins, or more

Topping:
½ cup icing sugar
⅓ cup butter or margarine
½ teaspoon vanilla
½ cup blanched shredded almonds (or other nuts, sunflower seeds, or coconut flakes)

Sift together the dry ingredients. Mix oil, egg, buttermilk, syrup, and raisins. Pour into the flour mixture, and stir rapidly but not long — like a muffin batter. Pour into a 9" x 9" pan. Cover with the blended topping mixture and bake at 350°F for about 35 minutes, or until a toothpick inserted in centre comes out clean.

SLICED APPLE COFFEE CAKE

This makes a pleasant treat on a frosty fall day.

2 medium-sized apples
1 tablespoon lemon juice
1½ cups flour
1½ teaspoons baking powder
½ teaspoon salt
⅓ cup butter or margarine
1 cup sugar
2 eggs
1 teaspoon baking soda
1 cup commercial sour cream (if you don't have the real thing)

Topping:
⅓ cup brown sugar
¾ teaspoon cinnamon

Wash, core, and slice apples (do not peel) and place in a bowl with lemon juice. Sift flour, baking powder, and salt together. Cream butter, add sugar gradually, beating well; beat in the eggs. Combine the baking soda with sour cream. Add to the batter alternately with dry ingredients. Blend well. Pour batter into a greased 9" x 9" cake pan. Sprinkle with ⅓ of brown sugar-cinnamon topping mixture. Spread apple slices on top and cover with remaining topping. Bake at 325°F for 45 minutes or until a toothpick inserted in centre comes out clean. Serve warm and it's wonderful.

EVA'S AUNT LOVINA'S CINNAMON-TOAST COFFEE CAKE

Light as a feather, and it really does taste like super cinnamon toast!

> 1 cup sugar
> 2 tablespoons melted butter, margarine, or oil
> 1 teaspoon salt
> 2 cups flour
> 2 teaspoons baking powder
> 1 cup milk
> 1 teaspoon vanilla
>
> *Topping:*
> 4 tablespoons melted butter
> 1 tablespoon cinnamon
> ½ cup sugar

Blend the sugar, butter, and salt, then add flour and baking powder, sifted together. Stir in milk and vanilla. Mix well. Turn into a 13" x 8" pan and bake at 325°F for 15 to 20 minutes or until golden brown. Now drizzle the 4 tablespoons of melted butter over the top, sprinkle over it the cinnamon and ½ cup of sugar mixed together. Return the cake to the oven and bake for 10 minutes longer. Eat it hot and eat a lot.

HONEY WHOLE-WHEAT COFFEE CAKE

Here's a healthy one that's easiest if prepared in a mixer, but the exercise of stirring and mixing might be better for you.

> 1 cup butter
> 1 cup honey
> 2 eggs
> 1 teaspoon vanilla
> ½ cup all-purpose flour
> 1½ cups whole-wheat flour
> 2½ teaspoons baking powder
> ½ teaspoon salt
> ⅓ cup milk

Topping:
½ cup brown sugar
1 teaspoon cinnamon
1 cup chopped nuts
⅓ cup wheat germ

Cream the butter and honey. Add the eggs and vanilla and beat well. Mix the dry ingredients together and add alternately with the milk, beating after each addition until smooth. Pour half the batter into a greased 13" x 9" pan. Blend the topping ingredients and sprinkle half on the batter. Spread remaining batter in the pan and sprinkle with the rest of the topping. Bake at 350°F for about 30 minutes. It's very nice.

MAPLE SYRUP COFFEE CAKE

This goodie could be used as a dessert.

1½ cups flour
½ teaspoon baking soda
¼ teaspoon cinnamon (optional)
¼ teaspoon cloves (optional)
½ teaspoon salt
1 egg, well beaten
½ cup sugar
½ cup buttermilk
¼ cup maple syrup
¼ cup oil
¾ cup chopped nuts

Sift the dry ingredients together — leave out the spices if you want more maple flavour. Blend the egg, sugar, buttermilk, syrup, and oil, then mix well with the dry. Pour into a greased 11" x 8" pan. Sprinkle with chopped nuts. Bake at 325°F for 35 minutes. Cool for 5 minutes before devouring it.

SHORTCAKE COFFEE CAKE

One evening when I was speaking to a Kitchener-Waterloo chapter of Beta Sigma Phi, Jody Jamieson told me she makes a super coffee cake by using the Strawberry Shortcake recipe in *Schmecks* and putting a good topping on it. She could easily use half the recipe but because it freezes so well she always makes the whole thing.

4 cups flour
2 tablespoons baking powder
1 teaspoon baking soda
1 cup sugar
1 teaspoon salt
1 cup shortening
2 cups buttermilk

Topping:
(see pages 52-53)

Sift the dry ingredients then blend in the shortening till the mixture is crumbly. Add buttermilk and mix just enough to make sure the dry part is moistened. Spread the dough in a 9" x 13" pan — or you can make half the recipe and put the batter into an 8" x 8" square pan. Sprinkle a good topping (see pages 52-53) over the top and bake at 400°F for about 20 to 30 minutes — prick the centre to be sure. Serve warm.

STRAWBERRY OR PEACH SHORTCAKE

For shortcake, you don't need the coffee cake topping. Simply sprinkle the top with sugar, then, when it is baked and cooled slightly, smother individual servings with strawberries or peaches.

People constantly stop me on the street and at the market or write to tell me this is the best shortcake they have ever tasted. I think so too. The dry ingredients and shortening can be blended in advance, the buttermilk stirred in at the last minute, and it can be baked when you want it.

FRENCH COFFEE CAKE

If you want to be fancy, this coffee cake is impressive and delicious but no harder to make than any other. I don't know why it's called French; in a dozen trips to France I've never seen or eaten anything like it.

½ cup butter
½ cup shortening
1 cup sugar
3 eggs
3 cups flour
1 tablespoon baking powder
1 teaspoon baking soda
½ teaspoon salt
1 cup sour cream
1 teaspoon almond extract
1 teaspoon vanilla

Topping:
¼ cup cocoa
½ cup sugar
½ cup chopped pecans or walnuts

Garnish:
¼ cup whole nuts (optional)

Cream butter and shortening. Beat in sugar, then eggs, one at a time, beating well after each addition. Sift flour, baking powder, baking soda, and salt. Mix sour cream, almond extract, and vanilla. Add flour mixture to egg mixture alternately with sour cream. Combine topping ingredients. Pour half the batter into a buttered tube pan. Sprinkle half the topping mixture over the batter in the pan, add the remaining batter and sprinkle with remaining topping. Run a knife through the batter just once for a marble effect. Bake at 350°F for almost an hour — but watch it after 45 minutes — or until toothpick inserted in centre comes out clean. To make this look really classy you might put a row of whole nuts around the edge of the top.

CATHERINE FROMM'S SOUR CREAM
COFFEE CAKE

Catherine used to be head dietitian in Eaton's Georgian Room in Toronto. This glorious creation was baking in Catherine's oven while we sat by her fireplace and made conversation as if we weren't aware of the tantalyzing aromas that wafted around us. Happy moment when we moved to the dining room for tea and demolished the whole cake while it was hot.

Topping:
**1 cup chopped nuts (I think Catherine's were
  mixed with cashews, if you want to be
  economical you could use toasted
  sunflower seeds)**
⅓ cup melted butter
⅓ cup white sugar
⅓ cup brown sugar
1 teaspoon cinnamon

Batter:
½ cup shortening
1 cup white sugar
2 eggs
1 teaspoon vanilla
2 cups flour
1 teaspoon baking soda
1 teaspoon baking powder
½ teaspoon salt
1 cup sour cream

Mix the topping ingredients first, then the batter: Cream the shortening and sugar, beat in the eggs and vanilla. Sift the flour, baking soda, baking powder, and salt and stir into the creamed mixture alternately with the sour cream. Spread half the topping mixture in the bottom of a well-buttered tube pan; spoon half the batter over it. Sprinkle the rest of the topping over the batter then spoon in the rest of the batter. Bake at 350°F for about 45 minutes till it is done.

While she was making the tea, Catherine let the cake stand for a few minutes before turning it out on a large cake plate to cool slightly before all of us had three generous portions apiece. It's so comforting to eat with fellow gourmands, or need I say gluttons?

FRUIT COFFEE CAKE

This is a Russian Mennonite coffee cake recipe: they call it *platz.*

1½ cups flour
1 tablespoon baking powder
1 teaspoon sugar
½ teaspoon salt
½ cup butter or margarine
½ cup table cream or whole milk
Fruit (plums, apples, apricots, or peaches)
    cut in segments

Topping:
1 cup sugar
½ cup flour
3 tablespoons butter

Sift together the 1 ½ cups flour, baking powder, 1 teaspoon sugar, and salt. Cut in the ½ cup butter as you would for pastry. Blend in the cream. Pat the dough into a 9" x 13" pan. Place fruit segments side by side on the dough and sprinkle with the crumbs made by blending together the topping ingredients. Bake at 350°F till golden. When cooled, cut in squares. If you like you may place your fruit neatly on the dough so that when it is cut in squares there will be fruit in the centre of each piece.

BLUEBERRY COFFEE CAKE

You can use frozen or fresh berries to make this delicious coffee cake.

> 2 cups flour
> 1 cup sugar
> 1 tablespoon baking powder
> ¼ teaspoon salt
> 1½ cups blueberries, fresh or frozen
> ½ cup oil
> 2 eggs, beaten
> 1 cup milk
> 1⅓ cups flaked coconut, or preferred topping

Sift dry ingredients. Gently stir in berries. Blend oil, eggs, and milk together, then stir into flour mixture. Spoon into an 8" x 13" pan. Sprinkle top with coconut or sugar blended with cinnamon or whatever you like. Bake at 375°F for about 25 minutes.

YEAST COFFEE CAKES

When we were very young, we knew no other coffee cakes but those made with yeast. Mother loved coffee cakes and baked them often, always four at a time: two to keep and two to give away. Over the years she must have given away hundreds. The keepers didn't last long; in our family of five, one would be gone at a sitting. But when Mother was living alone in the white house with green shutters she had built for herself after Daddy was gone, a coffee cake would often last for a week — with Mother enjoying it to the last stale crumb. I can still see her sitting at the end of her long kitchen daintily dipping the final slices into a cup of coffee and saying, "I know dunking isn't proper, but when you live alone you can do whatever you like."

MOTHER'S COFFEE CAKE

People who'd eaten them always said Mother made the best coffee cakes they ever tasted. They were light and moist, with a baked-on crusty brown-sugar topping that sometimes formed deep little wells of candy which we three sisters always jostled for and Mother usually managed to slice in half to satisfy at least two of us.

In **½ cup lukewarm water**, dissolve **1 teaspoon sugar**. Over the mixture sprinkle **1 tablespoon yeast**. Let stand 10 minutes.

Scald **1 cup milk**. Add **½ cup shortening**, **⅓ cup sugar**, **1 teaspoon salt**, and stir until the sugar is dissolved. Cool to lukewarm.

When cool, add **2 eggs**, the yeast mixture, and **1 cup lukewarm water**, (Mother used the water in which she had boiled potatoes). Add **3 cups all-purpose flour**. Beat mixture until smooth. One at a time keep adding **3 ½ cups more flour**, mixing well to make a soft dough. (Because Mother didn't like getting her hands sticky, she kept stirring and stirring, instead of kneading the dough.) She put the covered bowl of dough in a warm place till the dough had doubled, about 1 hour, then she divided it in 4, stretching and patting each portion to fit into greased cake pans (round, square, or oblong). Let the dough rise again till doubled.

Carefully, just before baking, Mother put on the topping:

¼ cup butter
1 cup brown sugar
1 tablespoon cornstarch
1 tablespoon cream, sweet or sour

Crumbs:
2 tablespoons soft butter
¾ cup brown sugar
¼ cup flour
A sprinkle of cinnamon

To make topping, melt butter over very low heat. Stir in the blended brown sugar and cornstarch and a bit of cream to thin the mixture. Gently spread topping over the puffy tops of the 4 coffee cakes. Mother then sprinkled them with the crumb ingredients and a sprinkle of cinnamon. (Sometimes for good measure, she would sprinkle a little handful of brown or white sugar over them as well.) Bake at 375°F for 30 minutes until golden. Watch them towards the last. The aroma of the coffee cakes baking is devastating. When we were young, we could hardly wait to get at them as they cooled on a rack. And often we didn't wait.

ONE AT-A-TIME COFFEE CAKE

It never occurred to Mother to freeze or refrigerate a coffee cake before or after baking it, as can be done with this cake. The dough can be divided to make three cakes — one to bake as soon as it's risen, the rest to keep in the fridge for up to a week and baked as you like.

> **1½ cups scalded milk, boiling water, or potato**
>   **water**
> **½ cup sugar**
> **½ teaspoon salt**
> **⅓ cup butter**
> **1 tablespoon instant yeast**
> **2 eggs**
> **6 cups flour**
>
> *Topping:*
> **(see pages 52-53)**

Pour the hot milk or boiling water over the sugar, salt, and butter. Let cool to lukewarm. Stir in yeast, eggs, and flour, blending thoroughly. The dough — or part of it — may now be put in the fridge for several days and used as you please.

When ready to use, let rise until doubled. Divide in 3 parts. Pat each section into a buttered cake pan and let rise again. Cover with the topping of your choice. Bake at 375°F for 30 minutes. (If you reserve some of the dough in your fridge, it must be allowed to rise before putting into pans and allowed to rise again.) Remove the cake from the pan and let cool on a rack before you slice it. Some people butter their slices of coffee cake but if your topping is rich enough it's not necessary.

BREAD-DOUGH COFFEE CAKE

Next time you bake bread, treat yourself to a coffee cake by stretching some of the risen dough to fit a greased cake pan; brush the top with melted butter and cover it with your favourite topping mixture (see pages 52-53). Let it rise again and bake at 375°F for about 25 minutes.

MARY'S PRUNE AND APRICOT COFFEE CAKE

Your guests will probably say this is the best coffee cake they have ever tasted. Baked in a tube pan, it is moist, delicious, and impressive.

¾ cup dried apricots
¾ cup dried prunes
1 cup milk
¾ cup sugar
½ teaspoon salt
2 eggs
½ cup softened butter
4½ cups flour, sifted
2 tablespoons dry yeast
½ cup lukewarm water

Topping:
⅔ cup brown sugar
1 tablespoon flour
1 tablespoon cinnamon
¼ cup melted butter
⅓ cup chopped walnuts

Pour enough hot water over the apricots and prunes to cover them. Let stand for at least 5 minutes. Drain the fruits and chop finely. In a large mixing bowl, combine milk, sugar, salt, and eggs and beat well. Add butter and 2 cups of the flour and beat until smooth. In a small bowl, sprinkle yeast over lukewarm water and stir until dissolved. Add yeast and 1 cup flour to milk mixture and beat for 3 minutes. Blend in remaining 1½ cups flour and chopped fruits. Pour a third of the batter into a well-greased 10-inch tube pan.

To make topping, combine brown sugar, flour, and cinnamon and sprinkle a third of it over the batter in the pan. Drizzle with a third of the melted butter. Repeat layers 2 more times then sprinkle walnuts over top layer. Let rise for about 1 hour, or until double in bulk. Bake at 350°F for 45 minutes or until done. Cool in pan for about 30 minutes then remove to a rack.

TOPPINGS FOR COFFEE CAKES

MOTHER'S TOPPING

This is the richest and the best topping — especially if it sinks into little wells of candy (see Mother's recipe, page 48). Actually Mother's topping could be divided to use either the first part or the second crumb part separately.

STREUSEL TOPPING

Combine ½ **cup brown sugar** and ½ **cup flour**, then rub ½ **cup butter** into the combination along with **finely grated lemon or orange rind** OR ½ **cup finely chopped nuts** OR **1 teaspoon cinnamon** OR any other flavour you fancy.

APPLE STREUSEL

Cover the raised coffee cake dough in the pan with finely sliced **apples**, brush them with **melted butter** and cover them with **Streusel crumbs (above)**.

SUGAR-CINNAMON TOPPING

If you want to be lazy, simply brush the top of the risen dough in the pan with **melted butter**, then sprinkle with **white or brown sugar** blended with **cinnamon**. It won't be as rich or as tasty but still quite acceptable.

NUT TOPPING

Combine thoroughly ½ **cup brown sugar**, ½ **cup melted butter**, ¼ **cup heavy cream**, and **1 cup chopped nuts**.

JAM TOPPING

Simply heat your favourite jam to lukewarm and spread it gently over the raised dough just before baking.

HONEY TOPPING

Blend together ¼ **cup soft butter**, ¾ **cup icing sugar**, and **3 tablespoons honey**. Sprinkle with nuts if you like.

OTHER TOPPINGS

Any of the toppings used for baking-powder coffee cakes could be used for yeast ones — or vice versa. Enjoy.

ROLLED OATS AND NUT STREUSEL

For a 9" x 13" cake, combine **1 cup brown sugar** with ¼ **cup flour, 1 teaspoon cinnamon, ½ cup butter, 1 cup rolled oats**, and **1 cup chopped nuts**.

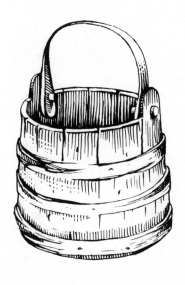

WHEAT THINS, CHEESE WAFERS, AND SAVOURY CRACKERS

Here's something I'm really excited about. One of the most interesting and practical discoveries I've made since I started writing cookbooks is learning how to make my own wheat thins, savoury crackers, and cheese wafers. They are so crisp, nutritious, and tasty that for me they've become an addiction. I never let my biscuit box stay empty longer than it takes me to whip up another batch of four or five different flavours.

I eat some every day with cheese, soup, dip, salad, or spread with cottage cheese blended with chives. If I'm not very firm with myself, I'll snack on them mid-morning or at bedtime. "No harm done," I rationalize. "They're not sweet."

It's great fun to experiment with various grains, flours, and flavours. I've made an infinite variety. Every batch is different and seems better than what went before. They don't look as neat, square, and perfect as those you buy in costly little boxes, but whenever I serve them my guests exclaim, "Aren't they good! I didn't know you could make things like this. I must have your recipe."

They are so quick and easy: you just mix them like pastry, roll them thin, slip the sheet onto an ungreased cookie pan, and indent the dough with a pastry wheel or a knife. I'm not good at figuring expenses but I'm sure they cost less than a quarter as much as the factory-made products; a batch with four cups of flour fills my round tin that is 8 inches across and 4 inches high. That's almost 200 crackers!

I can hardly wait till you try these and I get your reaction.

WHOLE-WHEAT THINS — BASIC RECIPE

From this basic recipe you can make biscuits galore, with as many flavours as you can imagine.

4 cups whole-wheat flour
1 tablespoon sugar
1 teaspoon salt (optional)
½ cup shortening
⅔ cup water or milk, more or less

Mix the dry ingredients. Cut in the shortening until it is finely blended. Pour in the water and stir till it forms into a soft ball, like pastry. (If you have a food processor all this can be done in a few seconds.) Divide the dough into 4 parts; roll each part as thin as parchment. (I roll mine on a lightly floured pastry cloth and it never sticks.) Slide the sheet of dough on an unbuttered cookie sheet and indent it in squares with a pastry wheel or a knife. To prevent bubbling, prick the dough all over with the tines of a fork — let it bounce.

Bake in a 400°F oven for almost 10 minutes, until crisp and pale brown. Slide the sheet to a cooling rack and break the biscuits where you have marked them.

Easy, isn't it? And you don't even have to wash the cookie pan.

DIFFERENT FLAVOURS

With one batch of the Basic Recipe you can make biscuits with four or more different flavours. After you have divided the dough, pat each piece into a ball, flatten it to an oval and generously sprinkle over it whatever flavour you please. Then roll the dough thin as you can and the flavouring will be smoothed out and rolled into it.

SAVOURY CRACKERS: Sprinkle the dough with **savoury salt.**

CELERY MORSELS: Sprinkle with **celery seed.**

SESAME SEED OR POPPY SEED CRISPS: Sprinkle with **sesame or poppy seeds.**

ONION NIBBLES: Sprinkle with toasted **onion flakes** — very popular — or **dehydrated onion soup.**

GARLIC GOBBLES: Sprinkle with **garlic powder or salt.**

CHIVE BITES: Sprinkle with **dried chives** or mix finely-cut **fresh chives** with the dough.

HERB TASTIES: Sprinkle with the herb of your choice.

BOUQUET GARNI BISCUITS: Sprinkle with a combination of herbs.

CAYENNE CRACKERS: Sprinkle with cayenne or paprika.

BEEF BITES: Sprinkle with beef bouillon mix or chicken broth mix.

Got the idea now? Just open your cupboard door and look around, make up your own names and your own flavours. It is surprising what you'll come up with.

SOY FLOUR SNACKS

The protein-seekers will find these a godsend; Nancy tasted them and said, "Oh good." Substitute **1 cup soy flour** for one of whole wheat in the Basic Recipe (page 55). Add any flavouring you like.

CRACKED WHEAT THINS

Pour a cup of boiling water over a cup of **cracked wheat, Red River Cereal, or 5-, 7-, or 12-grain cereal.** Let it soak for half an hour or so, then follow the Basic Recipe (page 55), using one less cup of flour. Add the soaked grain last; you might need a bit more water to get the right consistency. Add flavours if you like but they don't need them.

SOY NIPS

Using the Basic Recipe (page 55) substitute **2 or 3 tablespoons soy sauce** for as much water. The biscuits will be dark brown. Don't overbake them or they'll lose the subtle flavour and taste burnt.

WORCESTERSHIRE WAFERS

Substitute 2 tablespoons of **Worcestershire sauce** for water in the Basic Recipe (page 55).

SELEDA BAUMAN'S HOMEMADE CRACKERS

If you live in the country, you can't go shopping often. Because Seleda wouldn't be without crackers in the house, she made them.

**4 cups flour
2 tablespoons sugar
1 teaspoon salt
¼ cup butter
1 cup milk**

Sift the dry ingredients together, then cut in the butter until mealy. Stir in the milk to make a stiff dough. Roll out as thin as you can on a lightly floured surface; cut into squares with a knife or pastry wheel. Pierce each cracker with a fork, or simply dance a fork over the rolled dough before you cut it. Place on lightly greased cookie sheets and bake at 400°F for about 15 minutes, or until golden. Watch them.

THE ULTIMATE CRACKERS

After making dozens of batches of biscuits, I finally put in everything the nutritionists say is good for you. They are crisp, crunchy, with a toasty brown flavour having no need for embellishment.

> 1 cup rolled oats
> ½ cup bran
> ½ cup cracked grain
> ½ teaspoon salt
> ¾ cup margarine or butter
> 1 cup boiling water
> ½ cup wheat germ
> 1 cup sunflower seeds
> 1 cup whole-wheat flour
> ½ cup all-purpose flour

Measure the oats, bran, cracked grain, salt, and margarine into a bowl; pour in the cup of boiling water and stir till the margarine is melted and well blended. Let stand until lukewarm. Stir in the wheat germ, sunflower seeds, and flour. Proceed as in the Basic Recipe (page 55). This dough is a bit harder to handle but the result is worth the risk.

CHEESE WAFERS

These are tenderly crisp and deliciously cheesy — everyone's favourite.

> ½ cup margarine
> 2 cups flour, white or whole-wheat
> ½ teaspoon salt
> 1 cup finely grated cheese
> ¼ cup water, or slightly more

Blend the margarine with the flour and salt; blend in the cheese and gradually add as much water as you need to have the dough form a ball. Then do what the Basic Recipe (page 55) tells you. Watch them in the oven, don't let them brown. (Sprinkle them with sesame seeds or anything that won't detract from the cheese flavour. But why bother?)

CAPE BRETON OATCAKES

Wherever I've gone in Cape Breton I have been treated to oatcakes — golden, crisp, and more, more and morish. Mary McLeod at The Point in Ingonish was famous for hers: guests used to tuck them away in their pockets so they wouldn't have to wait till the next meal to get more. Miriam McLean, in The Bonnie House of Airlie near North Sydney, made fine oatcakes, too, and so did Clara May at Neil's Harbour. Jessie McEvoy who lives on a farm near Cape North served oatcakes with tea then took me to hunt crowberries behind the barn and beyond where she showed me the great field stones that mark the graves of her grandparents; she told me, "Instead of being buried in Dingwall graveyard they wanted to lie forever among their own mountains."

3 cups rolled oats
3 cups flour
1 cup brown sugar
2 teaspoons salt
1 teaspoon baking soda
1½ cups lard or shortening
¾ cup cold water

Combine all the dry ingredients. Cut in the lard then work it in with your fingers till it's really well blended. Add water a little at a time until the dough is right to roll, like pastry. Use rolled oats on the board instead of flour, and don't skimp it. Roll about ⅛-inch thin. Cut in squares with a knife and bake at 350°F for about 12 to 15 minutes. Watch them, they're too precious to let burn. Eat them with coffee or tea — or walking along a country lane by the sea.

DOUGHNUTS AND FRITTERS

Fresh homemade doughnuts and fritters are so good to eat, but dangerous to make unless you stay with them every single second that the deep frying fat is on the stove. Read your newspaper and find out how many house fires are started because someone walked away from hot fat. If your phone rings, turn off the heat before you answer; take the pot off the stove; let the doughnuts die a natural death, it's a small loss compared to losing your house or your life.

And never, never, put a lid on the hot fat pot. It can explode when you remove it. I have a friend who was horribly burned when he did it — and so was his kitchen.

Eva is lucky: she has three daughters to take over if there is a distraction when she is doughnut-making. In March before the men start boiling maple sap in the sugar bush, Eva makes more than seven hundred yeast doughnuts in a day. She tells me: "I make them and freeze them before I get busy canning syrup and making maple butter, then we eat some every day dunked in fresh syrup. We're all crazy for them."

When I call on Eva for syrup, she gives me some frozen doughnuts to take home. I put them in my freezer and allow myself to eat one a day until there are none. I selfishly never share them.

Doughnuts

EVA'S YEAST DOUGHNUTS

You can't buy doughnuts like these in a doughnut shop; you can have them only if you make them yourself or have a generous friend like Eva who always has some to serve with a nappie of maple syrup to dunk them in. They are light as a feather and the best in the world.

Eva uses Mary Ann Martin's No-Knead Never-Fail White Bread Recipe. If you don't want as many doughnuts as the recipe would give you, you could cut it in half or make as many doughnuts as you want and use the remaining dough to make a loaf of bread or buns.

1 tablespoon yeast
3½ cups lukewarm water
½ cup shortening
⅓ cup sugar
1 teaspoon salt
2 eggs, beaten
7 cups flour

Dissolve the yeast in ½ cup of the lukewarm water. Let stand 10 minutes. In a large bowl, pour remaining lukewarm water. Add shortening, sugar, salt, and eggs; pour in the yeast and mix well. Add the flour a cup at a time, beating well after each addition, until you have a soft dough. Cover the bowl, set in a warm place and let the dough rise until doubled — about 1 hour. Punch the dough down, pat out ⅓- to ½-inch thickness. Cut with a doughnut cutter or cut into squares or oblongs. Let rise, then slide one at a time into deep, hot fat (about 375°F). Each doughnut takes about 3 minutes to cook. Turn them as soon as they brown on one side. Never crowd too many in the fat at once. When done, drain on absorbent paper and serve hot. At a dessert party at Eva's we dunked dozens of them in maple syrup.

RAISED DOUGHNUTS

When you make bread or Kucha dough, take some of the risen dough and roll it into a sheet about ½-inch thick and cut it into rings or oblongs. Let stand until nearly doubled in size — fat and puffy, then fry in deep, hot fat (375°F). Drain on paper and roll in powdered sugar or eat with maple syrup. If you like, you can cut a slit in these and put in some jam or jelly. But why bother?

BEVVY'S DOUGHNUTS

Rich and very good.

> 1 cup sour cream
> 3 eggs, beaten
> ½ teaspoon salt
> 1 teaspoon cream of tartar
> 2 teaspoons baking soda
> Several cups of flour to make a soft dough

Stir all together in the order given. Roll ¾ of an inch thick on a floured board. Cut with doughnut cutter, and slide into hot lard (375°F) and fry till brown on both sides. Drain on absorbent paper. Shake in a bag with powdered sugar, or eat plain with syrup.

HONEY GLAZE FOR DOUGHNUTS

Instead of shaking doughnuts in a bag with powdered sugar, you could give them a glaze that makes them easier to eat without dripping powdered sugar down your front.

> 1 cup icing sugar
> 3½ tablespoons boiling water
> 1½ tablespoons honey

Stir all the ingredients till blended. Dip the warm doughnuts into the warm glaze and let cool and dry on a rack.

DOUGHNUT GLAZE

Here is another glaze that tastes good and is easy to do.

1 cup sugar
¼ cup milk
1 teaspoon butter

Boil all together for 2 minutes. Cool and add **½ cup icing sugar** and **1 teaspoon vanilla**. Dip doughnuts and let dry on trays or a rack.

ICED DOUGHNUTS

If you want your doughnuts to look store-bought, use a good butter icing.

MOTHER'S POTATO DOUGHNUTS

They have a delicate, different flavour and stay moist for days — not like most doughnuts that are good for only a few hours. This makes a lot of doughnuts. You can easily make half the amount, but after you've tasted them you'll wish you hadn't.

2 cups hot mashed potatoes
2 cups sugar
2 tablespoons butter
2 cups milk
1 teaspoon vanilla
Flour to make a soft dough — probably 5 cupfuls
5 teaspoons baking powder

Mix potatoes, sugar, butter, milk, and vanilla, then stir in the sifted flour and baking powder. Roll out ¾-inch thick, cut into small rounds, fry in hot, deep fat (375°F) until they are golden brown. Drain, then drop into a bag with icing sugar and shake till the doughnuts are coated.

FETSCHPATZE
Fat Sparrows

Called this, Bevvy says, because of the odd shapes they take when the batter is dropped in hot lard. I once ate nine at a sitting.

> 1 egg, beaten
> 1 cup sour cream
> Flour to make a stiffish batter
> 1 rounded teaspoon baking soda
> A little salt

You simply mix them up and drop tablespoonfuls of the batter into hot, deep fat (375°F). Let them become just past golden brown all over, drain them on absorbent paper for a minute or two, then see if you can resist less than nine — dunked in maple syrup.

FUNNEL CAKES

Bevvy's children always stand near the stove to watch the fun while she makes these.

> 3 tablespoons sour cream
> Not quite 2 cups milk
> 2 eggs, well beaten
> 3 cups flour
> 1 teaspoon baking powder
> ½ teaspoon baking soda
> ½ teaspoon salt

Measure the sour cream into a cup and fill the cup with milk, then stir the milk into the beaten eggs. Sift the dry ingredients into the egg-milk mixture and beat until smooth. If the batter isn't runny, you will have to add more milk. Heat deep fat till it browns a cube of bread, or reaches 375°F. Pour the batter into a small pitcher so it will be easier to handle.

Now comes the fun. Put your finger over the spout of a funnel and pour about 3 tablespoons of the batter into the funnel, take off your finger and let the batter run into the hot fat, swirling

the funnel around and around so the batter forms a lacy pattern
or concentric circles about 3 to 6 inches in diameter. Bevvy says
it's best to make the swirls from the centre out. The frying
becomes quite an art as you learn to make quick twists and turns
of the funnel, covering and uncovering the opening. It's not as
hard as it sounds.

Fry them until they are golden brown, drain them on paper
towels, and serve hot, sprinkled with powdered sugar.

Fritters

The longest line-ups at Elmira's Maple Syrup Festival early in April, at the Mennonite Sale in New Hamburg late in May, and at Wellesley's Cheese and Apple Butter Festival in the fall, are at the booths that make and sell hot Apple Fritters.

Fritters are a sort of doughnut with fruit in the centre — really special. You can make them with bananas, apples, peaches, or what have you.

When I was a little girl, Mother and Daddy had friends who came from Denmark. Mrs. Assmussen was a great cook and often made Prune Fritters that were unlike any others. Coated with sugar, they were fabulous. Of course, Mrs. Assmussen is dead and no one has her recipe. I've been trying for years to find it. If anyone in the world who reads this book knows how to make Danish Prune Fritters, please send it to me at R.R. 3, Waterloo, Ontario N2J 3Z4. You'd make me happy.

APPLE FRITTERS

When Mother made these we didn't want anything else that would waste our space.

   2 or 3 apples
   1 egg
   2 tablespoons sugar
   ½ teaspoon salt
   1 cup milk
   1 cup flour
   1 teaspoon baking powder

Peel the apples and carefully remove the core without breaking the apple; cut the apple into round slices about 1¼-inch thick. Beat the egg well, add the sugar, salt, then the milk alternately with the sifted flour and baking powder. You might need a bit more flour to make a fairly thick batter. Dip the apple slices into the batter, making sure they are well coated on both sides. Fry the rings in deep fat at 375°F till the fritters are golden all over. Don't prick them or they'll absorb fat; drain them. You may dust them with sugar and cinnamon or eat them as we did with maple syrup poured over them.

BEVVY'S EPPEL KICHLE
(Apple Fritters)

Instead of using the round, carefully cut slices of apple in her fritters, Bevvy chops up her apples — about 1½ cupfuls — adds them to the batter and stirs them in before dropping spoonfuls of batter into deep, hot fat.

FRUIT FRITTERS

This recipe was in a great grandmother's cookbook. Almost any kind of fruit may be used in fritters: apples, bananas, pears, peaches, plums, etc., are all suitable. Apples should be pared, cored, and cut into round slices about half an inch thick. They may be seasoned with a little lemon juice and nutmeg. Bananas should be cut into slices about an inch thick. Pears may be cut in quarters. Plums may be pitted with a lump of sugar replacing the pit.

> **2 egg yolks**
> **½ cup milk**
> **1 cup flour**
> **½ teaspoon salt**
> **2 teaspoons sugar**
> **2 tablespoons melted butter**
> **2 egg whites**
> **Fruit**
> **Icing sugar**

Beat the egg yolks till light and add the milk. Pour this on the flour and beat until smooth. Now add the salt, sugar, and butter; beat vigorously for 5 minutes. Set the mixture away in a cool place until it is time to use it. Prepare 6 large tart apples, or as many pears, peaches, bananas, or plums. Have lard about 3 inches deep in the kettle and very hot. Beat the whites of the eggs to a stiff froth and stir into the batter. Dip the slices of fruit into the batter, coating them thoroughly. Lift the fruit by passing a fork under it, and slide into the hot fat. Cook for 3 minutes till golden all over; drain on absorbent paper for half a minute. Arrange on a hot dish, sprinkle with icing sugar and serve immediately with a fork and dessert spoon.

BEVVY'S PASCHING PUFFA
(Peach Fritters or Puffs)

Peach Fritters served with whipped or ice cream make a super
dessert.

⅓ cup butter
½ cup sugar
2 eggs, well beaten
2 cups flour
1 tablespoon baking powder
½ teaspoon salt
1 cup milk
1½ cups chopped peaches, fresh or canned
½ teaspoon lemon juice (optional)
½ teaspoon vanilla

Cream the butter and sugar, add the eggs and beat together
thoroughly. Sift the dry ingredients together and add alternately with the milk. Fold in the peaches, lemon juice, and
vanilla. Slide by teaspoonfuls into hot fat (375°F) and fry until
golden brown. Drain on paper. Serve with whipped or ice cream,
or sprinkled with icing sugar.

BANANA FRITTERS

Mother usually made these for company and we had to finish
them up before bed-time because the bananas inside them
would turn black if kept longer. Happy day!

½ cup sugar
1 egg, beaten slightly
Pinch of salt
1 teaspoon maple flavouring
½ cup sour cream
1 cup buttermilk
Flour to make a stiff dough (try 2½ cups)
1 teaspoon baking soda
2 or 3 bananas
Icing sugar

Beat the sugar into the egg, add the salt, maple flavouring, and sour cream; then alternately add the buttermilk and flour sifted with baking soda to make quite a stiff dough. Cut bananas into ¾-inch slices, drop into batter, coat well and slide into hot fat (375°F) till nicely browned all over. Drain on paper and dredge with icing sugar. They're wonderful.

CORN FRITTERS

I could make a whole meal of these doused with maple syrup. You can see a picture of some I made on the jacket of my book Schmecks Appeal.

> **1 cup flour**
> **1 teaspoon baking powder**
> **¾ teaspoon salt**
> **2 eggs, beaten well**
> **¼ cup milk**
> **1½ cups corn, fresh, frozen, or canned**
> **2 teaspoons melted shortening**

Sift the flour, baking powder, and salt; combine the beaten eggs and milk and stir into the flour mixture. Add the corn and melted shortening. Drop tablespoonfuls into deep, hot fat (375°F) and watch them for 4 to 5 minutes till golden. Drain on absorbent paper. Eat hot and eat many.

CORN AND CHEESE FRITTERS

Add ½ **cup grated cheese** to the above recipe; it's good, too.

BATTERED ONION RINGS

Cut a Bermuda onion into ¼-inch slices; separate into individual rings. Dip rings into Basic Pancake Batter (page 72) and fry in deep fat. You might also experiment with mushrooms.

PANCAKES AND WAFFLES

There is so much written these days about the importance of nutrition. But don't feel guilty or worried if you make a whole meal of pancakes and maple syrup. Just don't do it often. You can balance your intake with fresh greens, vegetables, protein, and dairy products at other meals during the day.

Alone and in her own house, my mother lived to be ninety-one; she loved fresh bread and raspberry jelly and often that was her supper; but on those days she might have had leftover cucumber salad with a sour cream dressing for breakfast.

BUTTERMILK PANCAKES

In the spring when the sap is flowing and Eva and Hannah are busy putting freshly boiled maple syrup into cans, there is no better meal than tender, puffy pancakes swimming in syrup.

2 eggs
2 cups buttermilk
¼ cup vegetable oil
1¾ cups flour
2 tablespoons sugar
1½ teaspoons baking powder
1 teaspoon baking soda
½ teaspoon salt

Beat the eggs, then stir in the buttermilk and oil. Add the remaining ingredients. Stir just until all is moistened. Lightly grease a hot griddle. The temperature is right if a few drops of water sizzle and bounce when sprinkled on the hot surface. Pour a scant ¼ cup of batter in 4 places on the griddle to make 4 pancakes at a time. Cook until bubbles form on top and the edges start to dry. Turn over and cook on the other side.

If you want to be fancy, you could add fruit to the batter: a peeled, shredded apple, fresh or frozen blueberries, raspberries, sliced peaches, raisins, or currants. I like mine plain.

MAPLE SURUP

We in Canada don't seem to appreciate how privileged we are to be able to get pure maple syrup. Farmers go to a great deal of trouble to make it. Forty gallons of maple sap must be boiled to produce one gallon of syrup, which must then be pasteurized — boiled again — to preserve it in cans or bottles, which can be put on a shelf in your cupboard or fridge and used to enhance many things.

Remember, 1½ cups maple syrup 1 cup other sugar; in baking you might add ¼ teaspoon baking soda stirred into it — but I never bother, and things turn out very well.

Maple syrup poured over pancakes, griddle cakes, and waffles is, of course, a necessity. It is wonderful, too, as a sauce for puddings, or poured over ice cream or creamed cottage cheese. And for dunking doughnuts there is no parallel.

BASIC SWEET MILK PANCAKES

You can add other things to this batter if you want to.

    1½ cups flour
    2 teaspoons baking powder
    ½ teaspoon salt
    1 egg, beaten
    1 cup milk, more or less
    ¼ cup melted shortening — or vegetable oil

Sift the dry ingredients together; blend the egg, milk, and shortening and stir into the flour mixture just long enough to moisten. If you want thick pancakes, use less milk. If you want thin ones that you can roll up, add more — but don't beat the batter or the pancakes will be rubbery. Bake on a lightly greased griddle or pan, turning only once. Serve with heated maple syrup or any sauce you prefer.

You could vary this recipe by adding whatever appeals to you: cinnamon, nutmeg, seeds, herbs, sautéed onions, or cheese. Then serve with an appropriate sauce. My neighbour never serves pancakes without apple sauce, bacon, and sausages. There are other things.

MOCK MAPLE SYRUP

Sometimes on Sunday mornings at Sunfish Lake, we'd invite our neighbours for breakfast; I'd mix up a great bash of buttermilk pancake batter; my brother-in-law, Ralph, would bake the pancakes over an open fire on the lawn and twenty people would sit at our picnic tables and eat them smothered with maple syrup (they thought). Actually I had made the syrup the day before and no one knew the difference.

    6 cups brown sugar
    4 cups boiling water
    ½ teaspoon vinegar
    2 cups real maple syrup

Put the sugar into the boiling water, let the mixture boil for 5 minutes. When it has cooled, add the vinegar and real maple syrup; stir till well blended. You don't have to put in the real maple syrup but it does add flavour. When Mother made this, she used water in which very clean potatoes in their jackets had been boiled. Once she put in some maple flavouring, but the result was artificial.

WHOLE-WHEAT PANCAKES

Carol Hudgins is a nutritionist who likes to invent things that are good for her three children and her university professor husband, who looks very happy.

> **3 eggs**
> **Milk to fill 3 cups, including the eggs**
> **1 cup whole-wheat flour**
> **½ cup all-purpose flour**
> **2 teaspoons baking powder**
> **2 tablespoons sugar**
> **¼ cup bacon fat**

Beat the eggs in a 4-cup measuring cup, then add enough milk to make 3 cups. Pour the milk and eggs over the sifted dry ingredients and stir until the batter is lumpy-smooth, if you know what I mean. Fry in bacon fat in a 350°F frying pan. Serve with butter, maple syrup, and a wedge of lemon. Carol said her daddy always liked a bit of lemon with maple syrup. Also that a friend who had never liked pancakes liked these enough to eat six.

A nice touch, if you like, is to sprinkle sesame seeds or finely chopped nuts over the pancakes as they are baking and before you turn them over to be browned on the second side.

OATMEAL PANCAKES

With real maple syrup these are delicious. Better than porridge.

1½ cups rolled oats
2 cups milk
2 eggs
1 tablespoon brown sugar
1 teaspoon salt
¼ cup melted butter
1 cup whole-wheat flour
1 tablespoon baking powder
1 teaspoon cinnamon

Blend the rolled oats with the milk and let stand for about 5 minutes while you beat the eggs, add the sugar, salt, and melted butter. Stir in the oat mixture, flour and baking powder sifted together and cinnamon. Spoon a ladleful for each pancake onto a hot, lightly greased griddle or frying pan. Bake until the edges become dry and the surface is covered with bubbles. Turn and bake the other side. Eat immediately with butter spread over it and lots of maple syrup.

CORNMEAL PANCAKES

Great with lots of maple syrup poured over them.

1 cup flour
1 cup cornmeal
1 tablespoon baking powder
1 teaspoon salt
2 eggs
2 cups milk
¼ cup melted shortening

Simply combine all the ingredients and mix well. Drop spoonfuls on a hot, lightly greased griddle or frying pan, and fry until golden.

KEEPING TRACK OF RECIPES

Can you always find the recipe you're looking for? You know you used it last year but you can't remember which book it was in or where you put the clipping. Norm has five hard-covered notebooks in which she copies all the recipes she likes and uses. Now she never has trouble finding them. Bevvy Martin has a little black handwritten book. Eva and Hannah have several. Cathie Mathies, my neighbour who owns and operates a banquet hall keeps recipes she's clipped from periodicals under the cellophane-covered pages of books normally used for snapshots.

Since I've written my own cookbooks I have little trouble finding what I want or getting inspiration.

Why not try it? Write your own cookbook. You might even publish it for other people to enjoy.

HEALTHY APPLE PANCAKES

Try these in the winter when your diet could do with some uplift.

1½ cups whole-wheat flour
¼ cup wheat germ
1 teaspoon baking powder
1 teaspoon — or 2 — cinnamon
1 large apple, finely chopped (about 1 cupful)
2 eggs, beaten
1 cup milk

Combine the dry ingredients. Blend the apples, eggs, and milk. Stir apple mixture into the dry mixture until you have a smooth batter. Pour or ladle about ¼ cupful for each pancake on a hot, lightly greased griddle or pan and cook until the surface is bubbly. Turn over and cook on other side until golden brown. Serve with butter spread over each pancake and then smother it with maple syrup or applesauce.

ELDERBERRY BLOSSOM PANCAKES

This is a rare delicacy that can be had only during the brief days when the elderberry bushes are blooming — late in June or the first week in July.

Kitchener-Waterloo pancake enthusiasts spot in advance the wild elderberry bushes that grow along the country roadsides and, early in the morning while they are fresh, pick the clusters of blossoms, one for each anticipated pancake. Then hurry to the nearest picnic spot, make a fire, mix up a batch of pancake batter in a bowl, dip a cluster of blossoms, head first, into the batter and put it gently into hot shortening in a frying pan. While the pancake is cooking, the stem and veins are carefully snipped off with scissors, the pancake is turned and fried to a golden brown on the other side and eaten with maple syrup, bacon, and coffee. They have a nutty, almost meat-like flavour that is unusual and delicious.

SEEDS AND BANANA PANCAKES

My friend Sheila loves to experiment; she came up with this really good combination.

   1½ cups whole-wheat flour
   1½ teaspoons baking powder
   1 teaspoon salt
   1 egg
   1 tablespoon oil
   1 tablespoon honey
   1¼ cups milk
   1 large banana, sliced
   ½ cup sunflower seeds or chopped walnuts

Sift dry ingredients together; beat egg, add oil, honey, and milk; blend well, then add to dry mixture. Fold in sliced banana and seeds. Spoon batter onto hot griddle, brown lightly on each side and serve with honey butter or syrup.

NEIL'S HARBOUR BLUEBERRY PANCAKES

As soon as the blueberries were ripe on the barrens, Clara May would send the children with pails to gather as many as they could in an hour. They didn't mind doing it because they knew she would make them blueberry pancakes for supper. She made Brown Sugar Syrup (recipe follows) to eat with them because maple syrup was too expensive for her large hungry brood.

  2 eggs
  2 cups buttermilk
  1 teaspoon baking soda
  2 cups flour
  2 teaspoons baking powder
  1 teaspoon salt
  1 teaspoon sugar
  ¼ cup melted butter
  1 cup blueberries

Beat the eggs. Add buttermilk mixed with baking soda. Sift the flour, baking powder, salt, and sugar into the mixture. Pour in the melted butter, fold in the blueberries and fry on a lightly greased griddle or pan. Clara May always had to double the recipe — or make three separate batches.

BROWN SUGAR SYRUP

Clara May has to make two or three batches of this, too, when she makes pancakes.

  1½ cups brown sugar
  2 cups boiling water
  4 tablespoons butter

Boil all together — slowly — for about 10 minutes.

POTATO PANCAKES

To make these delicious, wonderful things as they should be made, you must have a wife, a maid, or a truly loving mother who will stand over the kitchen stove and fry them while you eat them as they come out of the frying pan, crisp, sizzling, and golden, with lacy brown edges. In our family, potato pancakes are the whole meal; we don't want anything else after we've each eaten at least a dozen, drowned in maple syrup.

5 or 6 medium-sized potatoes
3 eggs
5 or 6 tablespoons flour
1 teaspoon salt
¼ cup milk
Fat for frying

You must grate the peeled raw potatoes on the coarse side of one of those old-fashioned tin graters with rough holes; don't think you'll make it easy by using a shredder, food chopper, or grinder; they are too coarse, making the potatoes sloppy and starchy — I've tried all three and they don't work. You must grate the potatoes, always remembering as your arm becomes limp, that nothing in this world tastes much better. (Of course if you have a food processor you have heaven on earth.)

Put you must work quickly: don't let the potatoes stand when you've grated them or they'll turn rosy, then black, the starch will settle and you'll have an unusable mess. Stir up the grated potatoes, break the eggs into them, add the flour, salt, and milk.

Put 3 or 4 tablespoons of lard or vegetable shortening into a large frying pan; let the fat become hot, then drop small ladlefuls of the rather runny batter into it, spreading fairly thin in 4- or 5-inch rounds. Let them fry quickly — watch them every second; when the centre looks dry and the bottom is golden, turn them over and brown the other side. Slip them onto the plate of each eager eater who will be hovering round to devour them smothered in maple syrup. (My mother's German cleaning woman preferred hers with apple sauce, my neighbour has them with sausages — we think those are desecrations.) Don't, please, don't pile them up and keep them hot or they'll become limp and grey as an unbleached damp dish cloth.

ILE AUX COUDRES PANCAKES

When I stayed at L'auberge de la Roch Pleureuse on the island in the Saint Lawrence River near Baie St. Paul, I gloried in these thin delicious French pancakes smothered with Quebec maple syrup. They were served every morning for breakfast in the traditional provincial dining-room that faced the Laurentians. Beautiful.

  4 eggs
  2 tablespoons sugar
  Pinch of salt
  1 cup flour
  1 cup milk

Beat the eggs until foamy, add sugar, salt, and then the flour and milk, beating as you add, until very, very smooth. Heat a tablespoon of shortening in a smallish frying pan — about 8 inches across. Pour in enough batter to thinly cover the bottom of the pan — the thinner the tastier. Cook until brown on one side, then turn over and slightly brown the other side. Smother with maple syrup or roll up and spread with jam.

FLIP-FLAP GRIDDLE CAKES

Vary these good-as-they-are griddle cakes by adding ½ cup blueberries, or drained crushed pineapple, or sliced bananas, or fresh sliced strawberries.

  1¼ cups flour
  1 tablespoon baking powder
  1 tablespoon sugar
  ½ teaspoon salt
  1 egg, beaten
  1 cup milk
  ½ cup fruit (optional)

Sift the dry ingredients together. Stir in the egg and just enough milk to moisten. Add fruit gently — if you like. Bake on a hot griddle, turning only once to brown on both sides.

FRENCH CRÊPES

Every little village that Françoise drove me to in Brittany had a crêperie, and every town and city had several where only crêpes were served. But their variety was infinite. At a crêperie in Quimper there must have been at least fifty different kinds on the menu. Françoise ordered a poached egg in her first crêpe. I had cheese and ham; for dessert we had crêpes with fresh strawberries and one slathered with chocolate sauce.

Françoise's cook, Jeanne, always shuffling around in the kitchen in her flat felt slippers, often made great stacks of crêpes for Françoise's twenty-one-year-old son, Aimery, who was usually late for a meal at the dining-room table and liked eating crêpes, hot from the griddle in the kitchen. One day Jeanne made some for me while I sat at the kitchen table where she had put several pots of confiture — cherry, strawberry, peach, honey, and brown sugar — but no maple syrup. I made notes as Jeanne made crêpes.

> **2 cups flour**
> **¼ cup sugar**
> **3 large eggs**
> **½ cup cream**
> **2 cups milk**
> **2 tablespoons rum**
> **3 tablespoons melted butter**

Into a large bowl, sift together the flour and sugar. In a separate bowl, beat the eggs until light, then stir into flour mixture. Add the cream, milk, rum, and butter and beat until smooth. Let the batter stand at room temperature for 10 to 20 minutes. Heat a lightly buttered pan. The batter spreads in the pan. Jeanne helped it a little by tipping the griddle, so the batter covered all of it. The batter is so thin that the crêpes don't need turning.

FROZEN LEFTOVER PANCAKES

It's not likely that you'll ever have any pancakes left over, but if you do, put them on a cookie sheet and freeze them until they are stiff, then store them in your freezer in a plastic bag. They won't stick together. Pop them into the toaster to hot them up or in the oven. They'll be almost as good as new when you've doused them with maple syrup.

STRAWBERRY PANCAKES

The charming heritage Waterlot Restaurant in New Hamburg serves an incredible brunch every Sunday. After choosing whatever I liked from 30 to 40 different dishes on the cold buffet table, I ordered strawberry pancakes served with sausage, bacon, and a pitcher of maple syrup. Of course I couldn't ask for the recipe but I think any good pancake recipe (page 72) would do with sliced strawberries added to the batter just before baking.

WASHING UP

When I'm baking or cooking, I like to wash up dishes, pots, and utensils as I go along. I can't stand much clutter. I know some people who like to keep everything in sight; and I have one friend who won't even have her tea kettle on the kitchen counter when she isn't using it.

The window over my kitchen sink faces the lake so I prefer to do dishes in daylight when I can see what is going on there: ducks and a family of Canada geese swimming along, a kingfisher diving, canoes or swimmers passing by, or wind-surfers racing and falling, in winter, skiers or skaters. The window over my work counter, where I must concentrate, looks into the trees where only occasionally I look up and see little birds.

THE WAFFLE MAN

When we were very, very young the Waffle Man used to come round to the houses with his horse-drawn waffle wagon, where he made the waffles — hot and wonderful. Mother would run out to him with a plate and money. We'd eat the waffles doused in maple syrup before they'd get cold. And that was always a great day.

And somewhere — I don't remember where — Mother would buy us Waffle Sandwiches, warm oblong waffles with a ½-inch slab of ice cream between them, and Mother would say, "Now eat them before the ice cream drips on your good dress." And we did.

BASIC WAFFLES

I used to have a waffle iron but I gave it to Barbie; I've often wished I'd kept it because waffles can be such a treat.

> **2 cups flour**
> **1 tablespoon baking powder**
> **1 tablespoon sugar**
> **½ teaspoon salt**
> **2 eggs, separated**
> **⅓ cup melted butter or oil**
> **1¼ cups milk or slightly more**

Sift together the dry ingredients. Beat the egg yolks and stir them and the melted butter into the milk, then blend with the dry ingredients just enough to moisten. Fold in the stiffly beaten egg whites just before baking. Grease a hot waffle iron if you don't trust it without greasing. Pour in batter to an inch from the edge. Put down the top. Bake 3 to 5 minutes. Serve hot with melted butter and syrup or honey.

VARIATIONS

After you've proved yourself to be a pretty good waffle baker, you might try experimenting. You could try adding cooked **bacon bits** to the batter or:

1 cup canned corn — with less milk;
½ cup grated cheese — using less butter in the recipe;
½ cup chopped cooked ham folded in last;
½ cup finely chopped nuts, or raisins;
⅔ cup thinly sliced bananas — added last.
Personally, I like my waffles plain.

HAZEL'S SPICED WAFFLES

These are especially delicious with honey or maple butter.

1 cup flour
2 tablespoons sugar
1 tablespoon baking powder, slightly rounded
½ teaspoon salt
⅛ teaspoon cinnamon
⅛ teaspoon nutmeg
⅛ teaspoon allspice
1½ cups milk
2 eggs, separated
¼ cup melted butter

Sift the dry ingredients together. Mix milk with well-beaten egg yolks and add to the dry mixture. Stir in the melted butter then fold in the stiffly beaten egg whites. Bake in a hot waffle iron. Serve with soft honey butter or syrup.

RACHEL'S COOKED RICE WAFFLES

Keep cupfuls of cooked rice in your freezer for times when you want to make something special.

> **1 cup flour**
> **1 tablespoon sugar**
> **2 teaspoons baking powder**
> **½ teaspoon salt**
> **3 eggs, separated**
> **1½ cups buttermilk**
> **⅓ cup melted shortening or vegetable oil**
> **1 cup cooked rice**

Sift the dry ingredients together. Beat the egg yolks until creamy and combine with the buttermilk and shortening, then blend with the flour mixture. Fold in the rice. Beat the egg whites until stiff and gently fold into the batter. Bake in a hot waffle iron until golden. Serve with hot maple syrup into which you have beaten melted butter.

INDEX